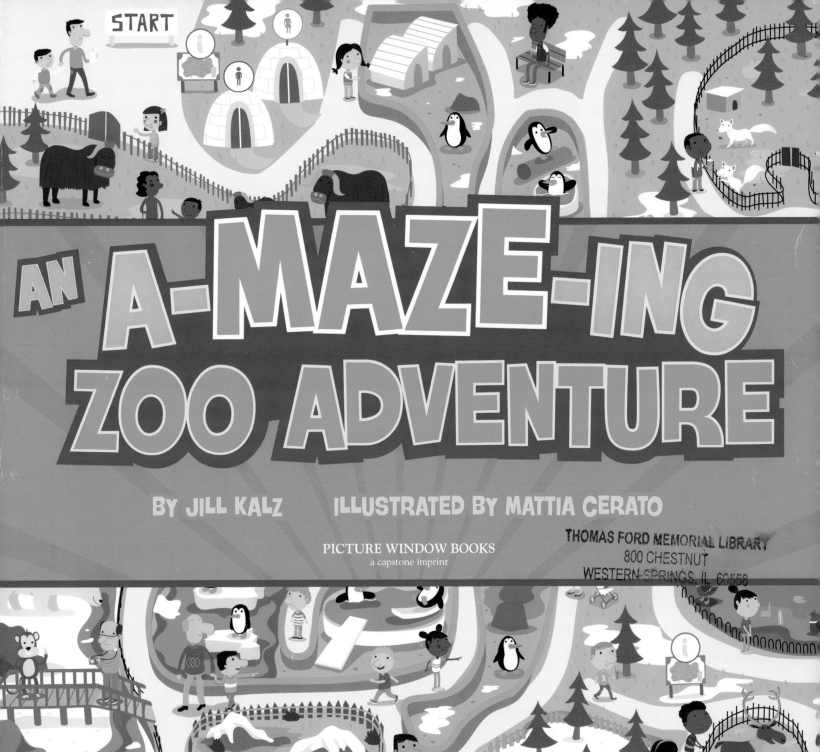

AN A-MAZE-ING ZOO ADVENTURE

BY JILL KALZ ILLUSTRATED BY MATTIA CERATO

PICTURE WINDOW BOOKS
a capstone imprint

Designer: Lori Bye
Art Director: Nathan Gassman
Production Specialist: Jane Klenk
The illustrations in this book were created digitally.

Picture Window Books
151 Good Counsel Drive
P.O. Box 669
Mankato, MN 56002-0669
877-845-8392
www.capstonepub.com

Library of Congress Cataloging-in-Publication Data
Kalz, Jill.
  An a-maze-ing zoo adventure / by Jill Kalz ; illustrated by
Mattia Cerato.
     p. cm. — (A-maze-ing adventures)
  Includes bibliographical references and index.
  ISBN 978-1-4048-6024-7 (library binding)
  1. Zoo animals—Juvenile literature. 2. Zoos—juvenile literature. 3.
Map reading—Juvenile literature. 4. Maze puzzles—Juvenile literature.
I. Cerato, Mattia, ill. II. Title. III. Title: Amazing zoo adventure.
  QL77.5.K343 2011
  793.73'8—dc22

                                            2010009866

Printed in the United States of America in North Mankato, Minnesota.
112010   005993R

WELCOME TO THE
A-MAZE-ING ZOO

Here's what you do: Use your finger to make your way through each maze from start to finish. If a person, tree, or other object blocks your way, choose a different path. It's OK to use the bridges and stairways. The star in the lower left corner of each maze shows direction. It's called a compass rose. The boxes with tiny pictures are called keys or legends. They'll help you find snack shacks, restrooms, shopping, and more.

What's that silly monkey up to? See if you can spot him sneaking through each maze.

Answers start on page 26.

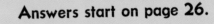

3

SOUVENIR

INFO

FOOD

START

4

Who's at the Zoo?

Look at all these animals! How many different kinds can you find? Which animals are east of the kangaroos? North of the penguins? Use the key to find the three gift shops.

KEY

⊗	Dining	🌽	Animal Feeder
🛍	Shopping	🗝	Lockers
👫	Restrooms	📷	Photo Spot
ⓘ	Information	✛	First Aid
$	ATM	?	Lost and Found

5

Outback Odyssey

From cuddly koala bears to wacky wombats, Outback Odyssey is home to animals from Australia. What building is west of the black Tasmanian devils? Can you spot the nine balloons? The five people with orange hair?

START

6

FINISH

FOOD

CLOSED

KEY

Dining

Restrooms

Shopping

Information

The Asia Trail

It's a jumbled jungle out here! Can you find all three information signs? Which animals are east of the gift shop? If you're standing by the bats, which direction do you have to go to see the turtle pool?

START

8

ATM

FINISH

KEY

Dining

Information

Shopping

$ ATM

Restrooms

Lockers

SHOP

9

African Safari

Whew! It's hot! Cool off with some ice cream. Is the dining hut north or south of the hippos? Can you find all five fat baobab trees? The elephants are east of which animals? Use the key to find the best photo spot.

START

GIFTS

SHOP

DINING

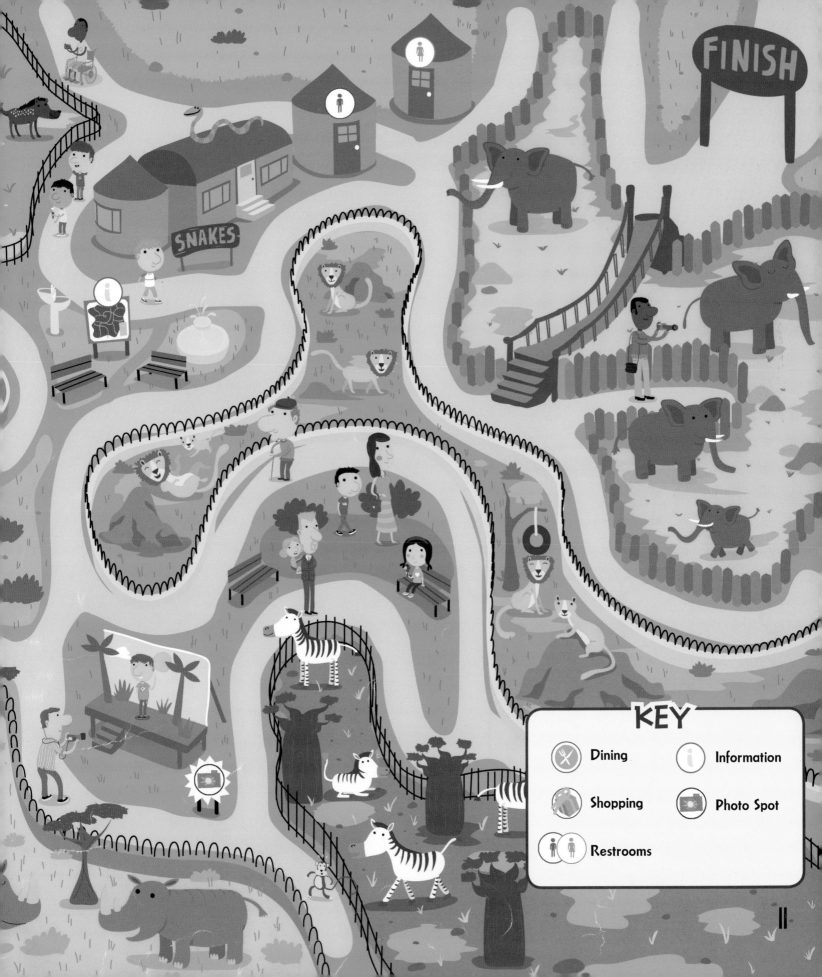

FINISH

SNAKES

KEY

Dining

Information

Shopping

Photo Spot

Restrooms

11

START

12

Discovery Island: Reptile House

Creep, crawl, and slither from start to finish. How many snakes can you find? Are the alligator and crocodiles west or east of the sea turtles? Which direction are the curly-tailed chameleons from the sleeping man?

FINISH

13

START

14

Discovery Island: Lights Out!

Too dark to see? Not for the skunks, ocelots, and other nighttime creatures that live here! Which animals are the farthest north? Are the owls west or east of the water fountain? Can you spot all six people wearing green shirts?

FINISH

15

Discovery Island: On the Farm

The petting zoo can be quite a puzzle! Which animals are south of the mini horses? Are the sheep west or east of the ducks? Which direction are the butterflies from the bunnies? Use the key to find all three animal feeders.

NURSERY

START

16

FINISH

DINER

KEY

Dining

Information

Restrooms

Animal Feeder

17

START

18

Polar Play

Filled with chilly thrills and icy surprises, Polar Play is a cool spot. How many information signs are there? Which building is west of the walruses? Are the caribou (reindeer) north or south of the arctic foxes?

FINISH

POLAR SHOP

IGLOO CAFE

KEY

Dining

Restrooms

Shopping

Information

19

LOST/FOUND

START

AMAZ🍴N CAFE

20

Rainforest Aviary and Monkey Land

Chirp! Chirp! Squawk, squawk! Squeal! Welcome to the noisiest part of the zoo! Can you find the seven benches? All 23 monkeys? If you're standing by the restrooms, which direction do you have to go to get to the Lost and Found?

FINISH

KEY

⊗ Dining	ⓘ Information
🛍 Shopping	➕ First Aid
🚻 Restrooms	❓ Lost and Found

START

BOOK SIGNING

ILLUSTRATOR
BOOK SIGNING

ZOO

Shop Till You Drop

Before heading home, be sure to buy a zoo souvenir. Can you find all four giraffe snow globes? The four baseball caps? Which items are south of the lollipops—the purses or the books?

Goodbye, Zoo!

There's only one way to the freeway. Find it before the traffic gets bad! Is the purple bus parked west or east of the motorcycles? What color is the car parked farthest north? Can you spot all three convertibles?

FINISH

MAZE ANSWERS

Who's at the Zoo? (page 4-5)

Outback Odyssey (page 6-7)

The Asia Trail (page 8-9)

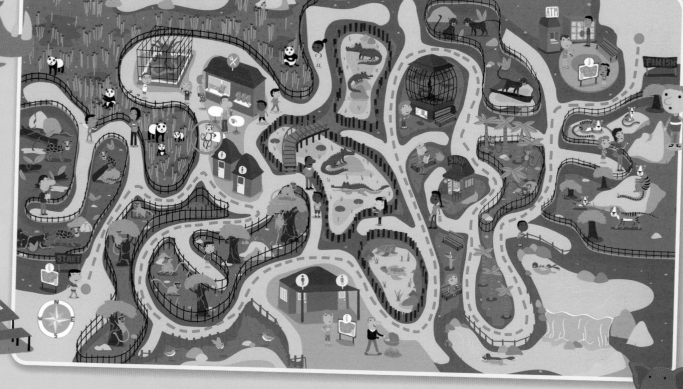

African Safari (page 10-11)

MAZE ANSWERS (continued)

Discovery Island: Reptile House (page 12-13)

Discovery Island: Lights Out! (page 14-15)

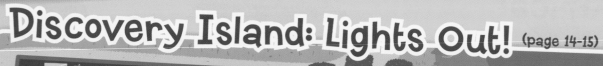

Discovery Island: On the Farm (page 16-17)

Polar Play (page (18-19)

MAZE ANSWERS (continued)

Rainforest Aviary and Monkey Land

(page 20-21)

Shop Till You Drop

(page 22-23)

Goodbye, Zoo! (page 24-25)

EXIT

START

FINISH

Back to the
ZOO

31

TO LEARN MORE

More Books to Read

Blair, Beth L. *The Everything Kids' Gross Mazes Book: Wind Your Way Through Hours of Twisted Turns, Sick Shortcuts, and Disgusting Detours!* An Everything Series Book. Avon, Mass.: Adams Media, 2006.

Munro, Roxie. *Amazement Park: 12 Wild Mazes.* New York: Sterling Pub. Co., 2009.

White, Graham. *Search for Pirate Treasure.* Amaze Adventure. Washington, D.C.: National Geographic, 2009.

Internet Sites

FactHound offers a safe, fun way to find Internet sites related to this book. All of the sites on FactHound have been researched by our staff.

Here's all you do:

Visit *www.facthound.com*

Type in this code: 9781404860247

Look for all the books in the A-MAZE-ing Adventures series:

AN A-MAZE-ing AMUSEMENT PARK ADVENTURE

AN A-MAZE-ing SCHOOL ADVENTURE

AN A-MAZE-ing FARM ADVENTURE

AN A-MAZE-ing ZOO ADVENTURE